Tricksters

Tricksters

PAUL COLLINS

Illustrated by Kevin Burgemeestre

Published by
Sundance Publishing
234 Taylor Street
Littleton, MA 01460

Copyright © text Paul Collins
Copyright © illustrations Kevin Burgemeestre
Project commissioned and managed by
Lorraine Bambrough-Kelly, The Writer's Style
Designed by Cath Lindsey/design rescue

First published 1998 by
Addison Wesley Longman Australia Pty Limited
95 Coventry Street
South Melbourne 3205 Australia
Exclusive United States Distribution: Sundance Publishing

ISBN 0-7608-3287-0

Printed in China

Contents

CHAPTER 1

It's Not fair!

"It's not fair! How come Katrina can have all her friends over for a slumber party, but I can't?" wailed Daniel.

"Because it would get too hectic," Daniel's mother replied.

"C'mon, Danny, be a sport. Our house is crowded as it is. Besides, you've got an appointment to go see the eye doctor later today."

"I don't want glasses like Bernard."

"Then you shouldn't sit so close to your computer screen."

"Well, can I go over to Jay's house?"

"And do what?"

"Homework."

Daniel's mother smiled. "Homework?"

"There's nothing else to do," Daniel whined. "Can I have a dollar to get some ice cream, then?"

"No, Daniel. If you must, go to your bedroom and play with the computer. We'll worry about you looking like Bernard later."

CHAPTER 2

Eavesdropping

On the way to his bedroom, Daniel heard squeals of laughter and hushed whispers coming from his sister's bedroom. He recognized the voices of Olga Valermis, Maria Conroy, and of course, his sister Katrina.

He paused by the door to listen, but moved away quickly. Somehow his sister always knew when he was eavesdropping.

"Daniel?" she called, her voice followed by a rush of hysterical laughter. "Daniellll . . . ?"

Back in his room, Daniel slumped down at his computer. He flicked through his games, *The Avenger's Own*, *Space Station Two-Zero-Five*, *The Pirates of Ghost Island*, and a new one, *Vampire Legends*.

The cover looked really gruesome. A claw-like hand had scratched away half of a castle, and blood was seeping from the cuts.

In Daniel's mind it all looked real.

"Daniel!" his mother called. "I'm going shopping. I'll bring you back a treat— your favorite, a meatball sandwich. Oh, and Daniel?"

"Yeah?"

"Don't scare yourself playing that silly vampire game. And leave your sister and her friends alone, okay? No pestering and no tricks!"

CHAPTER 3

Daniel's Plot

Daniel heard the door shut. "Don't scare yourself. Leave your sister alone," he echoed.

He stared hard at the cover of *Vampire Legends*. The cover had grooves in it with plastic tubing, and inside the tubing was . . . well, it had to be colored dye. But it *looked* like the real thing—blood.

More laughter rang out from down the hall.

Daniel looked hard at the game. He tilted it backward and watched the "blood" trickle throughout the castle ruins.

If *he* had been tricked into thinking it was blood, he knew the girls would believe it. He went into the kitchen and found a fork.

Daniel didn't like the idea of ruining the cover, but if it meant scaring his sister and her stupid girlfriends, it would be worth it.

21

Making sure not to tilt the game, he marched up to Katrina's bedroom and knocked on the door.

"Go away, Daniel," his sister called. Her girlfriends giggled.

"I've got something really weird here," he said excitedly.

"*You're* weird," Olga called, and the others laughed.

Katrina pulled the door open and glared at Daniel.

She looked at the game. "Go and play your silly computer game, Daniel. We're practicing how to put on makeup."

"Yeah, Daniel," Maria said from the bed. She made a face at him.

Daniel pushed past his sister and showed the game to the girls. "Look at this game—it almost looks alive!"

"It's just a silly computer game," Maria said, but she leaned forward anyway.

When they were all crowded around the game, Daniel pushed down hard on the plastic tubing. Red "blood" squirted everywhere from the holes he'd made with the fork.

Maria's scream was the loudest. Red ran in thick trails down her T-shirt. She jumped back, tripped on the bed, and fell.

Olga's eyes went wide, just like her mouth. Droplets of red splattered across her face.

"You're a brat!" Katrina yelled at him.

Daniel fled from Katrina's room, laughing so much his sides hurt. He headed downstairs to clean off the cover of his game.

CHAPTER 4

Creatures on the Loose

Katrina waited until she knew Daniel was out of earshot. She turned to her friends. "I know how to get him," she said. She picked up a stick of white makeup.

When Daniel returned from downstairs, he wiped his eyes with a handkerchief. That had been the most fun he'd had in ages.

He sat down at his computer and slipped in *Vampire Legends*.

He managed to get inside the castle really quickly. This game was too easy.

Now he was stalking the vampire. He held a hammer and a wooden stake in his hands. "Come out, come out, wherever you aaaare!" he called, as he moved through the dank passageways.

He moved the mouse quickly, brushing the side of the computer with his hand. He felt something sticky on his hand.

He looked down and saw a puddle of red. It looked like blood was oozing from his computer.

"Yuk!" said Daniel. He sniffed the red puddle. Whatever it was, it smelled terrible—like dead fish. "This is creepy," Daniel whispered.

Just then, from somewhere behind him, an angry voice snapped, "There he is!"

"Urgh!" Daniel screamed. He spun around. In his room, right next to him, were three scary creatures.

"Vampires!" he yelled.

Daniel's heart raced. His imagination went wild.

The creatures were wearing white, stained gowns. They had white faces with something trickling from their mouths and black, black eyes. One of them opened its mouth and rushed forward.

"Help!" Daniel screamed. "Help!"

They pounced on him. He fought back, but they were too strong. Two of them held him while the third one opened his mouth.

45

"Urgh!" spluttered Daniel. "Vampires!"

But instead of biting his neck for blood, somebody stuck something into his mouth. It tasted like month-old sardines.

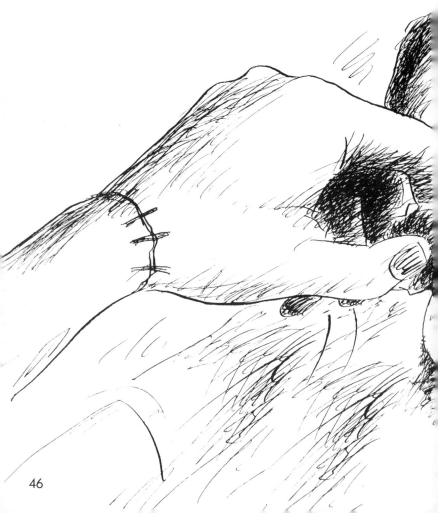

Tears sprang to Daniel's eyes. He tried biting down on the hand, but all he bit into was another mouthful of the same stuff.

The creatures held him down until Daniel
ate all of their disgusting food.

He was about to cry when they pushed him away.

"Hissss," they snarled at him. Then they were gone.

"Yuk!" Daniel moaned, trying to cough out the terrible food.

Mom Returns Home

He heard the front door open and close, then his mother's voice. "What are you girls up to? Get that silly makeup off, Katrina. It's not Halloween, and you look ridiculous."

"Daniel?" she called.

She poked her head into his bedroom, just as he was wiping his face on his T-shirt.

"Daniel, it smells dreadful in here. Air out your room and then come eat the meatball sandwich I brought you."

"I can't eat," Daniel groaned. "Three vampires attacked me. They fed me something awful. I feel *really* sick."

"Oh, Daniel, those vampires were Katrina and her friends. I told you to leave the girls alone—but you couldn't resist. So they decided it was time to trick the trickster."

She laughed, "Maybe I should take you to that eye doctor's appointment right away. At least then you'll be able to see the difference between your sister and a real vampire!"

ABOUT THE AUTHOR

Paul Collins

During Paul's early years in school, his teachers often accused him of daydreaming. He says that everything he is writing now has been thirty-odd years in the making. He would like to meet those teachers again, if only to prove that he wasn't daydreaming at all. Rather, he was making up stories for when he left school!

Daydreaming aside, Paul has edited several books for younger readers, including the award-winning *Dream Weavers*, the *Shivers* series, and his latest, *Fantastic Worlds*.

Paul's own books include *The Wizard's Torment*, *Old Bones*, *The Hyper Kid*, *The Shadow Factory*, *Spaced Out!*, and *Rude Cars*.

He encourages kids to daydream—but not around teachers!

Kevin Burgemeestre

Kevin was born in Australia and has studied art and design and illustration. He works out of his own studio, which he shares with his enormous collection of car magazines and his two-year-old son, Jim, drawing, drawing, drawing . . .

Kevin illustrates books and prepares weekly collages for a magazine. When he illustrates with ink, Kevin uses a dip-in mapping pen in a loose, friendly manner. For his colored illustrations, he works in either water color with soft washes or strong color gouache applied with sponges. Kevin's collages reflect his passion for movies and cubism, and sometimes end up as sculptures.